GOODNIGHT
LITTLE
PANDA

by Sinoun Blomfield

Illustrated by Elizabeth Ravets

by Sinoun Blomfield
sinounblomfield@ymail.com

Illustrated by Elizabeth Ravets
https://www.instagram.com/matilda_ravets/

Little Panda, no need to fuss.

He opens wide for his toothbrush.

And hops in the bath so he can play.

With little ducky swimming all the way.

His little bath is warm enough.

It's bedtime, Little Panda.

He puts his toys away.

And puts on his PJs.

In his little bed.

It's time to stay.

Hush now, Little Panda. It's time to go to bed.

Sweet Panda dreams will fill his head.

Mama sing a lullaby so he'll be alright.

Mama and Papa kiss him goodnight.

Whoosh! the wind blows.

Little Panda, is very scared.

Little Panda, is unprepared.

It's dark and scary.

But have no fear, Mama and Papa are very near.

Papa plugs in a bright night light.

Mama gets a stuffed toy for him to snuggle tight.

Little Panda stretches and yawns.

Happy that his fears are gone.

Little Panda, it's time to say goodnight.

COLORING
PAGES

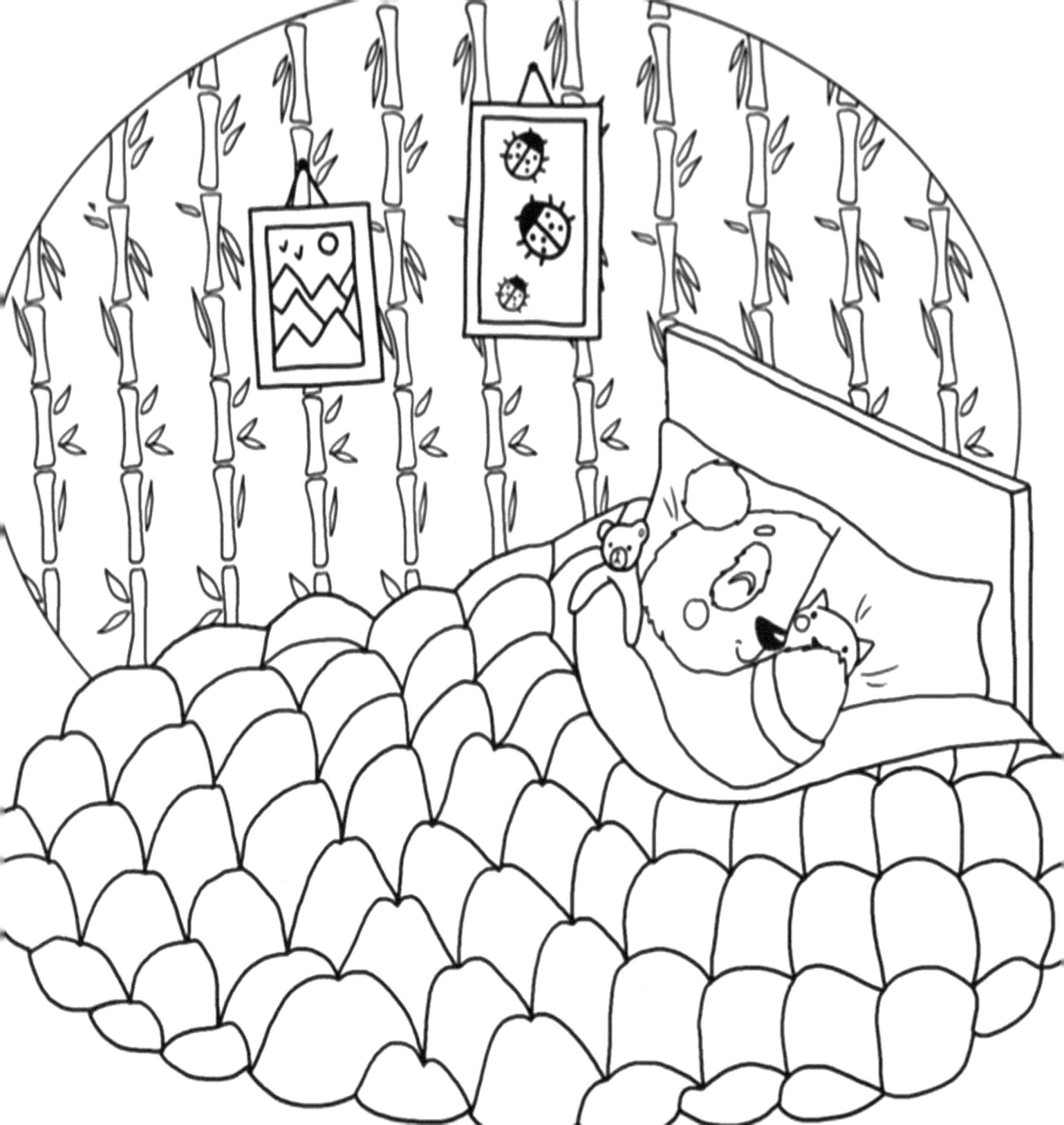